AF504397

CONSTANCE MITCHELL STANDS UP

Print ISBN: 979-8-3302-8196-1
Digital ISBN: 979-8-3302-8195-4

Published by IngramSpark

First Edition, Printed in 2024

This is a work of nonfiction. The events, people, and places described are real, based on the true story of Constance Mitchell.

Illustrated by Shawn Dunwoody

Constance Mitchell Stands Up

By Leslie C. Youngblood with Constance Mitchell-Jefferson,
Dr. Walter Cooper, and Shane Wiegand

Illustrated by Shawn Dunwoody

Constance Jenkins was born in New Rochelle,
New York, on May 19, 1928. No one knew
what an important leader she'd become in
Rochester, New York, 300 miles away.

Her courage would inspire Rochester residents
to stand up for their rights and help make
the city and the world a better place.

Having been raised by her mother and grandmother,
Constance's early life was full of strong and
determined women who were her role models.
When she wasn't playing with other kids or doing
her chores, Constance loved books full of adventure.

Little did she know that her real life would
prove to be full of unexpected twists and
turns—some great and others frightening.

SERVANT to Mr. JOHN
P O E M S
ON
OUS SUBJECTS,
RELIGIOUS AND MORAL
BY
PHILLIS WHEATLEY,
NEGRO SERVANT to Mr. JOHN WHEATLEY,
of BOSTON, in NEW ENGLAND.
LONDON:
Printed for A. BELL, Bookseller, Aldgate; and sold by
Messrs. COX and BERRY, King-Street, BOSTON.
MDCCLXXIII.

At 10 years old, Constance was on
her way home from school when
a car struck her. Luckily, someone
rushed her to the hospital.
She was in a coma for six months
before making a full recovery.

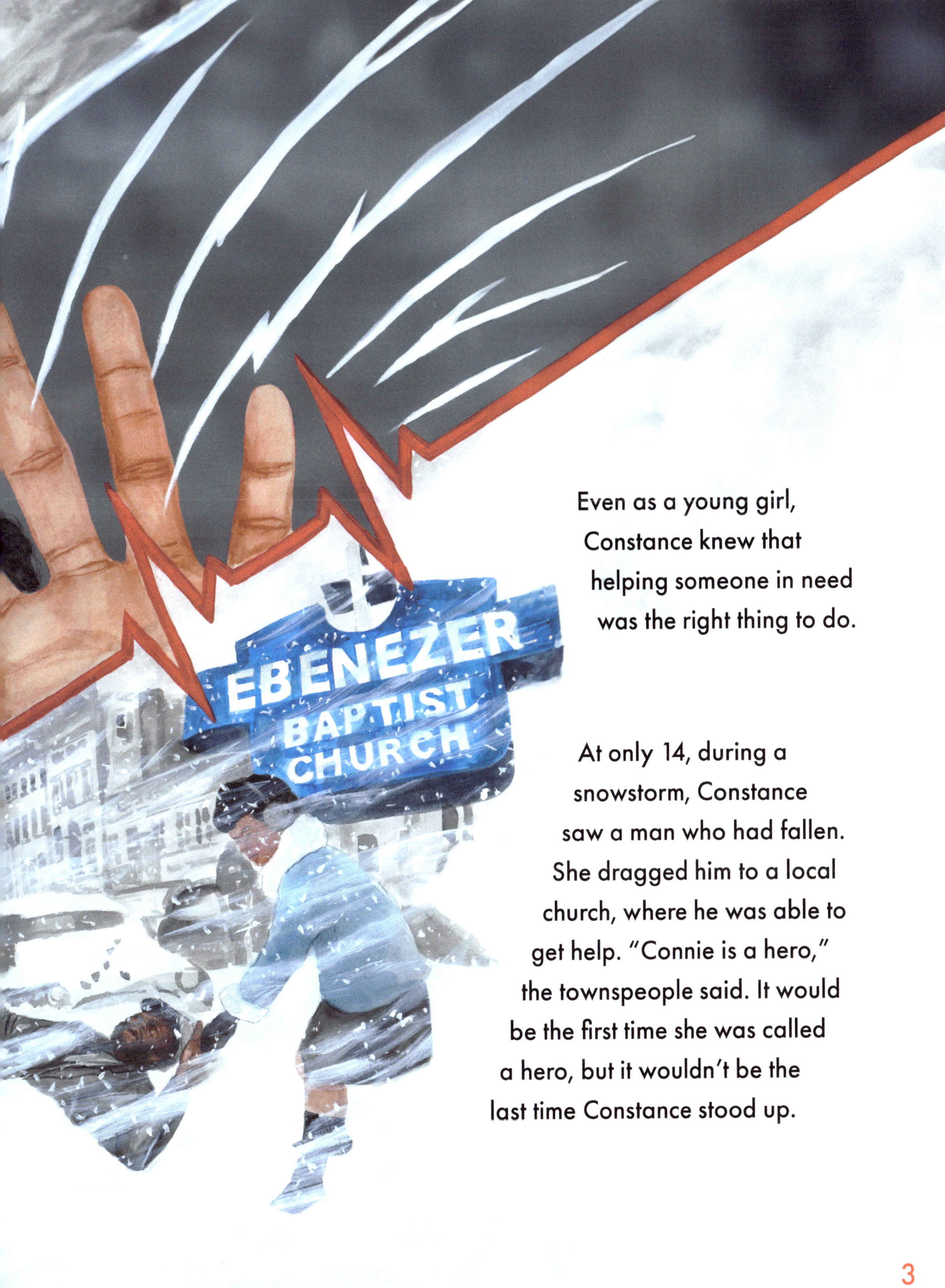

Even as a young girl, Constance knew that helping someone in need was the right thing to do.

At only 14, during a snowstorm, Constance saw a man who had fallen. She dragged him to a local church, where he was able to get help. "Connie is a hero," the townspeople said. It would be the first time she was called a hero, but it wouldn't be the last time Constance stood up.

After Constance finished high school, her family couldn't afford to send her to college right away. She used this time to explore different skills. Shampoo girl, salesgirl, and secretary were a few of her jobs.

4

She was never afraid of hard work.
These jobs allowed her to interact
with people, which she enjoyed.

But Constance found time for fun, too.
She loved to dance. Twice a month, she
and her friends would attend dances
at the YMCA. At one dance, when she
was 21, she met John Mitchell.

After a courtship, which included
Constance's grandmother tagging along
on one date, Constance and John married.
Shortly after, in 1950, they moved to Rochester.

Constance thought Rochester was
a beautiful city, but she and John
noticed big problems, especially
in Black neighborhoods. Instead
of moving away, they stayed
and decided to make it a
better place. The Mitchells
were ready to stand up.

And there were others ready to get to work. Constance volunteered at the Baden Street Settlement House. Together, they helped farmworker children, who didn't have running water or safe spaces to live, learn to read. They tutored adults, too.

However, access to education was only one of the problems. Constance always had a stable home. Many in Rochester, and its surrounding areas, didn't.

And growing up in New Rochelle, she wasn't used to the separation of Black and White neighborhoods that she witnessed in Rochester. That was a problem because the Black neighborhoods were overcrowded.

WELCOME
CHESTER

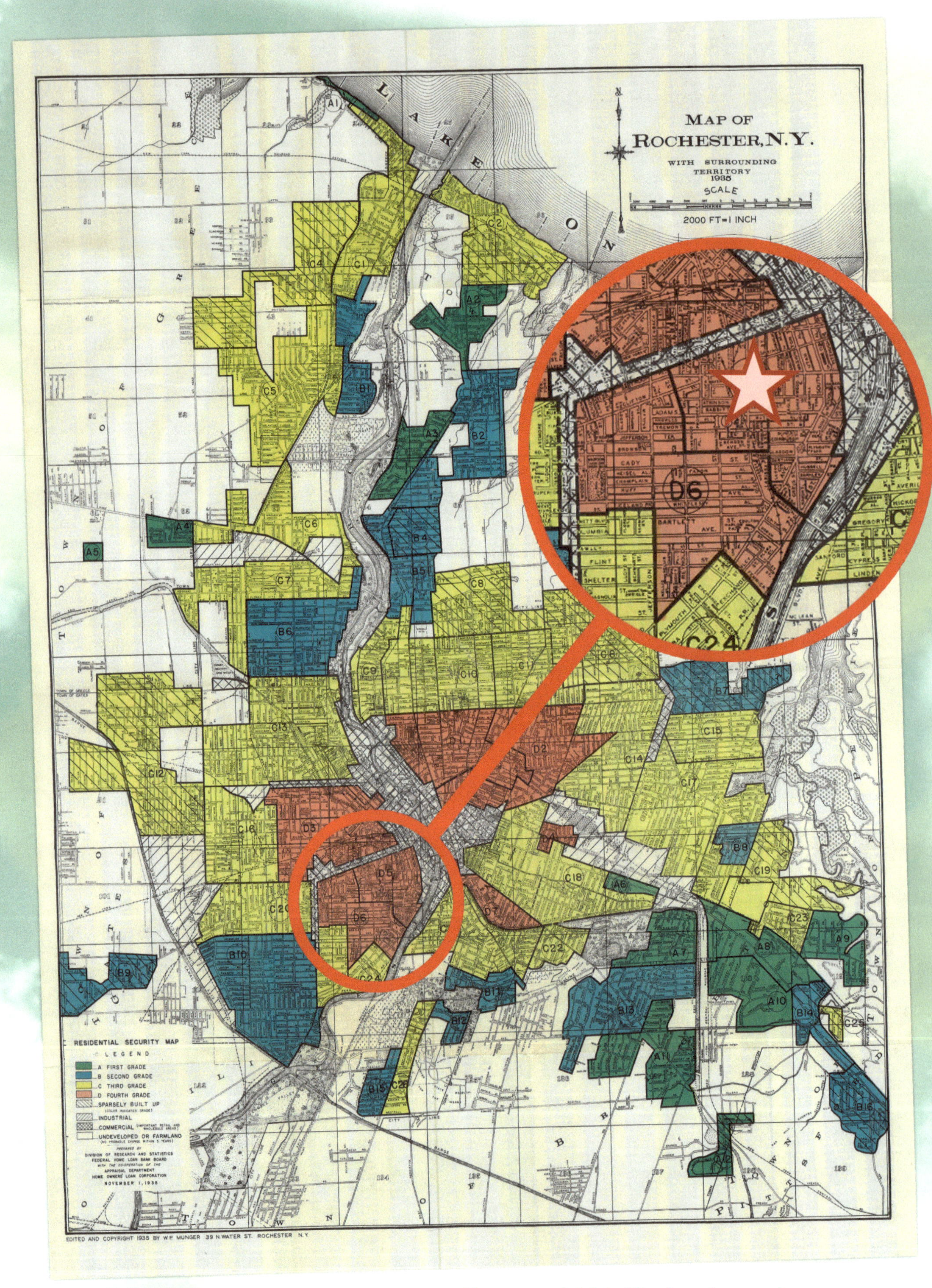

Constance's Neighborhood in Rochester, NY

One day, Constance said to John,

"City officials, real estate agents, and bankers are only allowing Black people to live in two neighborhoods. That's redlining."

John agreed. And they vowed to do something about it.

Sometimes four or five families lived
in one house that didn't have running
water and had dangerous pests.

White property owners collected
rent but didn't repair the
houses. That wasn't fair!
And it got a lot worse.

Several people were
hurt in raging fires.

Even when Constance was sad, **she stood up!**

She turned that sadness into action. Along with other community leaders, she wrote letters to the local newspaper.

Constance wanted the entire city to know what was happening in her neighborhood.

She didn't want the property owners to get away with such bad treatment of Black people.

But there was someone in charge of Constance's
neighborhood who didn't care about Black people:
a White man named Lester Peck. "People, not houses,
make slums," Lester Peck said. He even blamed the fires
and bad housing conditions on the Black people.

"That's racist. We can't let this Peck stay in charge! He has to go!"

Constance said to her friends, which now included members of
a social action club. They all agreed, but they were too afraid
to challenge Peck. Because they were Black, they could lose
their jobs. Constance gathered her courage and stood up!

Constance Mitchell was scared, but she knew she had to
stand up and fight for the people who deserved better.
In 1959, with the encouragement of her friends, and
support of her husband, Constance entered the election
for Supervisor of the Third Ward, the neighborhood where
she lived. She did the best she could, but she lost.

Losing didn't mean she wouldn't try again. She even had
someone else to fight for: her daughter. She wanted Little Connie
to have the best possible future. Sometimes, when Constance
knocked on doors, she'd carry her daughter with her.

★ ELECT ★
CONSTANCE MITCHELL
149
DEMOCRATIC CANDIDATE
FOR
SUPERVISOR 3rd WARD
★ VOTE ROW "B" ★

Constance had a magical way of drawing
people in. Most of all, she worked hard
to earn the trust of her neighbors.
She brought the jar of coffee, a can of
milk and a bag of sugar, and would say,

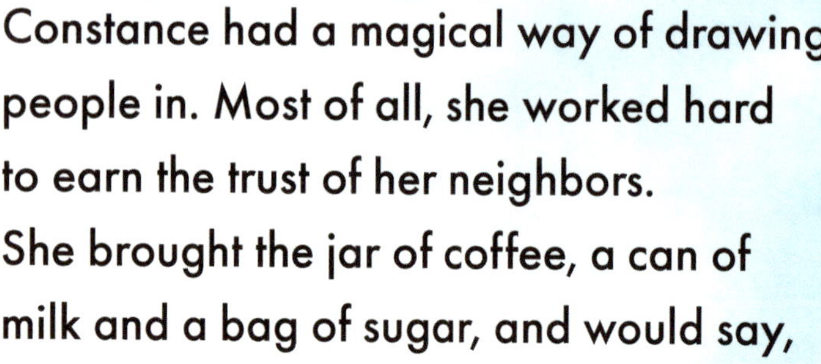

"As long as you have a cup, we are all set."

Sometimes they
didn't have a cup but
together, they always found
a way to make it work.

She won her next election!

We Demand
THE R...
STOP
BRUTAL...
ALABA...
We Demand
THE RIGHT
TO VOTE
EVERY-
WHERE

Constance's impact was important in Rochester and in any place where people were fighting for their rights.

One of those places was Selma, Alabama, more than a thousand miles from Rochester. In 1965, John and Constance Mitchell traveled to Selma to march with Dr. Martin Luther King, Jr., several other civil rights leaders, and a sea of everyday people who wanted the right to vote for all Black people. The trip to Selma made her eager to return to Rochester and do even more to help her community.

When the Mitchells
returned, their home
became a meeting spot for
community and world leaders.

One of the most
recognized visitors was
Malcolm X, who shared
the same birthday as
Constance. They discussed
how to help Black people.

Constance wanted Rochester to become a city where Black people had the same opportunities as Whites. In 1994, she helped the first Black mayor of Rochester get elected, William (Bill) A. Johnson, Jr.

Constance Mitchell said in a newspaper interview,

"We've come a long way in the fight against racism, but we still have a lot more standing up to do."

After a life of service to the world, especially Rochester, Constance Mitchell died at the age of 90.

The best way we can keep Constance Mitchell's memory alive is for every resident to do the best they can to help make Rochester a better place.
Are you ready to do what you can?

WHAT WILL YOU STAND UP FOR?

Learn more about Constance Mitchell

No matter where she worked or who she helped, Constance never stopped standing up for what was right.

In 2017, Constance Mitchell received the Frederick Douglass Medal for Outstanding Civic Engagement for standing up against racism and fighting for better housing conditions in Rochester.

And her daughter, now Constance Mitchell Jefferson, whom Constance had carried with her throughout the community, was there to witness Constance's achievement.

Constance's daughter wants readers to know that her mother had a sense of humor. When she relaxed at home, one of her favorite meals was pasta, and sometimes Brooklyn-style pizza. One of her favorite quotes was, "Good. Better. Best. Never let it rest until your good is better than your best." That's the way she lived her life.

GOOD. BETTER. BEST. NEVER LET IT REST UNTIL YOUR GOOD IS BETTER THAN YOUR BEST.
Frederick Douglass Medal
FREDERICK DOUGLASS MEDAL
ABOLITIONIST · HUMAN RIGHTS ACTIVIST · ORATOR